Amazon FBA
How To Sell On Amazon And Become Prosperous

Table of content

Introduction

Selling on Amazon doesn't need to be difficult. It's actually possible to sell a lot of products, in a short amount of time, without a whole lot of effort. Of course, you're going to have to put a little work in to get started, but if you follow along with these tips we're going to help you make more money. It's only going to take a few simple steps to get you started and then you'll be able to continue using these tips to build a successful business.

Amazon is a great platform for selling just about anything and if you follow along with these tips you're going to be able to make the most of it. Don't let yourself flame out as a business just because you don't know the tips and tricks of the best and brightest that Amazon has to offer. So let's get started on the path to you being able to sell more products and make more money than you ever thought possible.

Chapter 1 – Using Competitive Pricing

Since there are so many different people and businesses that you can purchase from, it's important to make sure that you are using some type of differentiating factor. In this chapter we'll talk about using competitive pricing. We'll explain why you definitely want to check out your competition and make sure that you're keeping your prices lower than the competition. After all, price is one of the most important factors when a potential customer considers you and your competition.

The first thing you should do when you are putting up products is look for other products that are similar to yours. For example, if you sell electronics you will want to look at other companies that also sell electronics on Amazon. This way you'll be able to see what the costs are for some of the specific products you may be interested in posting. You'll then be able to see which prices the products are actually selling for and what price they seem to be just sitting in stock. You want to make sure that your products sell.

Next, make sure that you are pricing your products not just to sell but to compete with even the lower priced products on Amazon. You don't have to be the lowest price on the site. What you want is to be comparative to the lowest price. When your prices are comparative you have a better chance of being chosen when someone starts shopping for your products.

Of course, it's important to consider some of the important exceptions to this rule. For example, if another company is selling the same product you are at a cheaper rate but they have a lot of negative reviews you don't need to match them as closely. After all, negative reviews are going to cut down on the amount of people willing to purchase from that particular person.

Another exception is if your product is not exactly like the other ones being offered. If your product is slightly better or slightly newer you'll be able to increase the price slightly. These are two reasons that you can consider making your products more expensive, but remember that you shouldn't increase the price by a lot unless your products qualities far exceed what others have to offer. If there aren't enough improved qualities you won't be able to get the higher price as no one will see the value.

Chapter 2 – Instate a Pro Merchant Subscription

There are a number of different benefits to having a pro subscription through Amazon. Of course, you don't have to get a pro subscription and can instead continue selling through an individual account; however, you will have to pay 99 cents per transaction. With a pro subscription you pay a flat rate of $39.99 per month but nothing at all per transaction.

If you consider a fee of 99 cents, for example, you'll only have to sell 41 products to get your money back. After all, after 41 products, at an individual rate, you'd have spent $40.59. So any products after that 41 will be earning you even more money than you would per product on an individual account. With a pro subscription instead, you'll be able to keep that additional 99 cents each for the products above and beyond 41. If you're selling a lot of products per month you definitely will want to consider paying the fee. Outside of the monetary benefits, that fee will get you:

1. Bulk Product Upload – If you have an individual account you have to upload items individually. This takes a lot of time and effort and you'll have to continue maintaining your entire catalog of products one by one. If you have a pro account you'll be able to use spreadsheet templates to help you upload all of your items at the same time. This makes the entire process simpler.

2. Better Sale Management Reports – When you use pro subscriptions you'll be able to get a lot of additional reports that don't come with an individual subscription. This means you'll be able to keep track of your sales even better and understand the products that are selling best and when. This will help you understand which additional products you should sell or post.

3. More Options for Selling/Prices – For an individual account there are lower price limits. If you have a pro account on the other hand you'll be

able to price your items much higher. In this way you can post much larger products and sell them for the prices that are required.

4. Ability to Upload New Types of Items – Yet another difference is that pro users are capable of uploading items that individual users are simply incapable of. You'll want to look into the specific types of items that are allowed with an individual account and which are specifically allowed for pro users.

Chapter 3 – The Ability to Automate Listings

Yet another benefit that you can get on Amazon (but only as a pro subscriber) is to automate your listings. You will be able to list a number of items all at the same time (through the bulk feature mentioned above) and the entire process is automated so you don't have to worry about managing a lot of things like inventory or product descriptions. All of these things are going to take care of themselves.

The great thing about being able to automate your listings is that you don't have to worry about problems with counts of how many items you have in stock or changing listings to reflect new items. You also don't have to worry about getting onto your computer constantly to make sure that all of your items are working properly on Amazon. Instead, all of these things are taken care of for you. They're also taken care of for all of your products at the same time instead of having to work on each one individually.

You don't even need to create your own automated module. Instead, you can use one of the premade ones that will help you fill in the blanks with your information and then post it in only a few simple steps. Once you've posted, making changes is also a simple process as well and all your changes in the template will be uploaded automatically to the website itself. You don't have to worry about checking each individual piece.

Chapter 4 – Product Marketing

Yet another way you can improve your abilities on Amazon is to use product marketing. There best thing you can do is improve the chances that someone who has purchased from you once is going to do so again. This can actually be done quite easily. All you need to do is provide them with some type of deal after they have made a purchase. You can actually do this in a few different ways, depending on the type of products they are purchasing.

If the customer has purchased something they will need again, such as dog food, you can provide them a coupon to get their next bag for a certain percentage off or for a lower price. If they have purchased something they won't need for a long time you can offer a discount on something they may be interested based on that product. For example, if your customer has purchased a dog cage they may be interested in dog accessories (such as a collar, leash or bowl) as well. You can offer them a discount off one of these types of products.

By sending a coupon for another purchase you are increasing the odds that your one-time customer will turn into at least a two-time customer. After that second purchase you can still send them offers but they don't have to be quite as good. If your service and products are good, then after a couple great products they will be willing to continue purchasing from you even at full price. This means you've made yourself a longer term customer that's more likely to talk about you.

Another method of improving your sales is to use those repeat customers. You can send a different type of coupon to customers who have purchased from you at least once allowing them to get bigger discounts if they refer friends. These coupons are actually an even better deal for you. Let's say your dog bowl sells for $5.00. It costs you $2.50 to make that bowl and market it. So you make $2.50 off each dog bowl.

Now if you give a customer a coupon for $2.00 off a dog bowl you will only make .50. That's not a very good profit margin. If, instead, you give them $2.00 off a dog bowl if they refer a customer you will have a higher profit margin. Let's say (for arguments sake) that dog bowl is the only thing you sell. So you sell the dog bowl to your referred customer for $5.00 and to your repeat customer for $3.00. You personally have just make $3.00 off two dog bowls instead of only .50 off one. It's definitely an improvement in your profit margin.

You may even want to consider offering a smaller discount for referring one customer (such as .50 off or $1.00 off) and increasing the discount amount for additional referrals.

Chapter 5 – Use Fulfillment By Amazon

You may not think that this feature is a benefit to you as you'll have to spend a little more money in order to use it, but it's actually going to help you a lot. Think about how much time each day you have to spend going through your orders, finding the items, packaging them up, taking them to the post office and shipping them. All those steps are definitely going to take you time and energy. They're also costing you money.

Now if you use fulfillment by Amazon you don't need to spend that time and money. What you do is send all of your products to Amazon's warehouse. Once your items are received they will catalogue everything and make sure it's stored properly. When those items are purchased they find the items, package them and ship them for you. You don't have to pay anything extra for boxes or filler or tape or shipping costs because that's all part of your fee.

The added benefit is that you don't have to worry about the time wasted in boxing and shipping. Plus you'll get a notification if your products are running low so you can ship out a whole bunch all at once again. It's a much easier process for you and it works pretty well for Amazon too. Plus a lot of people prefer buying products that are fulfilled by Amazon because they get them faster, they often get free shipping, and they can get a better guarantee.

Chapter 6 – Make Sure You Play Fair

There are a lot of rules to selling on Amazon and you're required to follow all of them. If you aren't careful you could find yourself breaking a rule and that can get you banned. Obviously that means you aren't going to be making any money and that's going to ruin your chances of being successful through Amazon.

Reading through all the rules is going to take you a lot of time and effort but it's important. You won't possibly be able to follow all the rules unless you read them because there's just too many and they cover a lot of small details. So you want to make sure that you check out Seller Central and the help area. This is going to let you look at all the different policies.

If you break a policy you may get a warning (depending on what type of policy you break). But if you break too many rules you'll find yourself getting suspended or even completely banned from the site. Some of these rules may not be what you'd expect which means it's even more important to read through everything. If you don't you may break a rule without even realizing it or meaning too. Unfortunately, you'll still get punished the same as if you intentionally broke the rule.

Chapter 7 – Be the One in the Buy Box

When someone searches anything on Amazon they will get one result that is higher than all the rest. Just like when you're building a website, you want to be the number one result on the search. That's because most people assume that number one on the search results is the best choice. You want to make sure that you are that number one result.

There are a couple things you can do to make sure that you show up as number one. The first is to make sure that you are the lowest price. You have to make sure that you include the cost of shipping in that price to make it lower because if someone else is offering their products through the fulfillment center their shipping costs are nothing. That means if their price is at all lower than yours it will come up first. The unfortunate thing is that their price without shipping is being compared to your price with shipping.

That means if your cost for the item is $24.99 plus shipping of $4.99 for a total of $29.98 and their cost without shipping is $28.98, they are considered cheaper than you, even though your product cost is actually cheaper. That's because the complete cost is lower.

Now another thing to do is make your product unique. If it's different from other products then you'll have a better chance of making that buy box as well. This can be done through bundling more than one product to make a pack or by creating a unique bundle of different items that work together. This will almost always guarantee you the buy box and help you get even better results on searches.

Finally, you can have a completely unique item. This means that whenever someone searches that item you're the only one who sells it so you automatically show up as the number one option to buy from.

Chapter 8 – Always Communicate Effectively

Whenever you sell items on Amazon there will be a method for others to communicate with you. This can be done directly or indirectly. If someone sends you a message it's important that you respond very quickly. Amazon asks that you respond within 24 hours but the faster you can respond the better it's going to look to the customer.

This is especially true if they have a question or concern about your product. If they have questions you want to answer them quickly so they will purchase. If they have a concern you want to take care of it quickly so they'll leave you good feedback.

Now customer questions will show up on Seller Central so you don't have to worry about missing anything. If you're really concerned you can even have the messages forwarded to a cell phone or your email so that you can communicate quickly and easily with any customers or potential customers.

Another way that customers can communicate with you is by leaving feedback on your products. You want to make sure that you are answering feedback as well. It may seem strange but it's actually important.

If you have any bad feedback you want to answer this publically so that everyone else who reads through your feedback to buy your product knows that you take care of any problems that arise. If you respond to positive feedback it shows that you value your customers and their opinions.

Chapter 9 – Ship Fast and Track it

If you decide not to go with the fulfillment center from Amazon you'll have to ship out items yourself. This may not seem like a big deal but it's actually quite difficult to keep track of everything that is ordered in one day and get it ready and out to your customers. Even more, you need to make sure that you are sending out everything very quickly.

Your customers know that it could take a couple days to ship out their products but they don't really like this. While you most likely won't get *bad* feedback for making your customers wait a couple days before you ship your products out, you won't get *great* feedback either. What you'll get is completely average.

Now if you ship out all products within one business day it means that your customers are going to get their products faster. That's definitely going to improve their reviews because they really want that product. That's why they ordered it after all. So when you ship the product fast they are even happier. If you provide a tracking number so they can see where the product is and when it will show up this improves their opinion of you even more.

These two small things may not seem like much (and they aren't required) but you will definitely improve your ratings and your feedback from customers. Plus they will improve the rate of return customers, referrals and recommendations.

Chapter 10 – Keep Featured Seller Status

The most important thing is to keep your featured seller status. If you have at least 95% positive reviews on Amazon you'll be able to stay in the featured seller zone. This means that your products are perfectly safe and you are safe as well. Your account is not going to get shut down (unless you break one of the other rules or policies which we already recommended you read up on).

If you fall below that 95% positive rating you'll start getting into a little trouble and some danger. You want to make sure that you're keeping your feedback and status up higher because this is going to ensure that you get to keep selling and keep making money.

This is another reason it's important to respond to negative feedback. Now we mentioned making sure you respond publically but you want to make sure you respond to these types of feedback privately as well. The reason you respond publically is so that others can see that you make sure to take care of problems and improve your look to others who may be considering purchasing your products.

When you respond privately you want to make sure you're making the situation with the customer right. You want to make sure you're doing something to help them such as sending an immediate coupon or gift card and an apology. Make sure you request more information about what the problem was and how you could make it right.

Once you receive information about the problem you'll be able to do whatever you can to improve the situation. Try to make them happy and you can even request that they remove their negative feedback. If they do it will help to improve your ranking again. If they don't, it's publically shown that you wanted to fix the problem and that you contacted them to do so. Either way it helps to make you look better to new customers.

Chapter 11 – Use Your Keywords Accurately

Whenever you list a product you need to make sure that you are creating a product description. This is going to help anyone looking at your product understand what it is, what it does and why they have to have it. You want your product description to be great so that when someone reads it they decide that they absolutely have to have that product and that they really want to get it from you.

Before your customer gets to the point where they are reading your product description however, they will search for something in the search bar. In order to get your product to the top of that search bar you need to make sure that your keywords are accurate and common as searches. If you have the best words to describe your product but no one ever searches those words you're just going to have a lot of great products sitting in storage somewhere.

When you list items you will list keywords that are going to be used to find your product. Amazon allows you to select a range of different keywords but you need to make sure that you select high performing words. Amazon won't tell you that. So the key is to make sure that you find a quality search tool.

You can use Google's keyword tools to help you find some of the highest searched keywords or you can use other applications like Merchant Words to help you find other successful keywords. In this way you'll be able to make sure that when someone searches they find the products you have to offer.

Chapter 12 – Don't Run Out of Product

Your products need to be in stock in order for you to get excellent rankings for your sales. Those rankings are going to improve your ability to sell additional products so it's important to keep rankings high. Unfortunately, you need to keep your rankings high on every product that you have in order to make sure that you are keeping your ability to sell as high as possible.

Now when your product inventory runs out that means you can't sell the product. Your product sale ranking is based on when you last sold the product and how many sales you've made. When the product is out of stock your last sale because further and further in the past. For each day that your product is out of stock the number continues to sink and it's extremely hard to get those numbers back up.

What you need to do is make sure that your products don't fall out of stock. This requires you to keep close track of everything that you sell and to make sure you're monitoring your inventory so that you can replace products as they start getting low. This way you can make sure that your products aren't ever out of stock and your rankings don't dip because of preventable problems.

You can help yourself with this by using the Replenishment Alert tool along with Amazon's fulfillment center. This will allow them to alert you whenever you products are getting low. Plus you get to set the quantity that you want to be alerted at. That way you can make sure you can get the product in quickly enough to always be in stock.

Chapter 13 – Fulfill Order Properly

If you're not going to use the fulfillment center or even if you are, you'll need to ship products. If you don't ship products properly they could be broken or damaged through the process of shipping. This will cause products to be sent back and it could result in some negative feedback from your customers. Even if you send replacement items right away it can be a problem for customers and they are likely to complain.

What this means is you need to make sure that you are fulfilling orders the right way. First, the most important thing is to ship the item that was ordered. If you're shipping to an individual you need to make sure that you send them the item they wanted. Sending the wrong item will get you very bad feedback. If you're sending to Amazon you need to make sure you label the item properly so they know what to do with it when it arrives.

The next thing to do is make sure that you are packing the item so that it doesn't break in transit. This means using the right types of boxes, wrapping each item, using packaging materials and making sure that there is some cushion around the item. Even if the item shouldn't be breakable you want to make sure you're following these rules to keep it safer.

By keeping your products secure you're improving the chances that it will arrive safe and sound and that your customers will be nothing but pleased.

Chapter 14 – Increase the Average Selling Price

One of the best ways to improve the money you make is to improve your Average Selling Price. Now you always have to pay some fees when you use the fulfillment center but they will be flat fees. One is for order handling and one is for pick and pack. Now you don't pay a lot for these fees but they are there. Now in order to offset that you want to make sure that you're getting as much money per product as possible.

Your average selling price is the price that you receive after you pay those fees for the product. So you want to make sure that for every low priced item you have for sale you're also selling some higher priced items. This helps to offset the price that you are paying to Amazon and you're able to make more money per item.

Your average selling price takes all items into account which means if you sell an item that makes you $3.00 after fees and one that makes you $40.00 after fees your average selling price is $21.50. You want to get this number as high as you can because that's how you actually make the most money possible. This would mean you were making even more money.

Now you'll need higher priced items to continue to increase your average selling price but don't get so caught up in high priced items that you neglect items that are priced lower but selling in high quantities. If you can consistently make $500 a month selling an item that only sells for $15 each you're going to want to keep that item. Even though the profit margin after fees is lower than an item that sells for $50, you may not sell as many of that $50 item.

Chapter 15 – Use Multiple Images

Using images is definitely going to help you sell your products. People like to see items before they buy them. Now when buying from a website that means they don't get to actually touch or see the item in person and they want to make sure that it's going to be exactly what they want. The more expensive the item the more they want to check it out and make sure it's just right.

If you post multiple pictures from different views and different angles it's going to improve the chances of someone choosing your item over another. They will be able to evaluate the item you have to offer and they'll feel more confident that it's the one they really want to choose.

Make sure that when you post images you're also using the right standards according to Amazon. They will tell you the size and quality you should have for images and that's going to ensure that your listing isn't taken down or your pictures aren't taken down. It's also going to allow your customers to have a better view of the product.

Chapter 16 – Solicit More Reviews

One of the best things you can get on Amazon is reviews. You want to get as many positive reviews as possible compared to the number of sales that you have. The more positive reviews the more additional people are going to purchase your product. So by getting positive reviews you're helping yourself earn more money and helping more people make great choices to buy those products.

Getting reviews isn't always easy however as not everyone is interested in leaving feedback. Some people just want to purchase their product and then not be concerned with anything else. On the other hand some people just don't think leaving a review is that important or they forget about it. That's why you want to make sure that you ask for feedback.

Wait a week or so after your product arrives to your customer and send them an email. It doesn't have to be extremely personal but make sure you use their name and the product they bought. Ask if there were any problems with the purchase or if there is anything you could do to make it better and then ask for them to leave a review if they really enjoyed the product. Make sure you even include a link to take them to exactly where they need to be.

By asking for a review your customers will be more likely to leave one and the easier you make it for them the better the chances. This is going to improve your sales dramatically.

Conclusion

Hopefully all of these tips were informative for you. When you put them into practice you're definitely going to notice a lot of benefits in selling more products and making more money. You're going to get a lot of excellent feedback as well which is only going to improve both of these things. Make sure that you're doing everything you can to help yourself.

If you really want to make a living selling products on Amazon you need to make sure you're following all these tips. It's going to make your life much easier and it's definitely going to make you a more successful business.